The New Brazil Travel Guide

Eco Tourism, Social Entrepreneurs, and Inspiring Adventures through all five regions

by Richard Brownsdon

The New Brazil Travel Guide

Eco Tourism, Social Entrepreneurs, and Inspiring Adventures through all five regions

A percentage of author royalties are donated to our partner projects that preserve and protect land in the Amazon Rainforest.

Thank you for your purchase and support.

For more information or to contact the author, please go to www.RichardBrownsdon.com

Table of Contents

Introduction

You hold in your hands a new type of travel guide. A guide told in stories.

Through it, you'll discover how you can have the adventure of a lifetime in Brazil.

This guide will connect you with some of the most fascinating people that live in this land. It will show you some secret places that not even a Brazilian would know of.

No matter the region you are visiting or the length of your stay, you'll learn how to make the most of any Brazilian adventure.

You'll read stories of eco-tourism and social entrepreneurship from all corners of this vast country.

In Part 1, as we travel around the country we'll discover five timeless truths from inspired individuals that you might come to think of as Brazil's guardian angels.

In Part 2, we'll take a look at your five steps to eco-travel success in Brazil. From connecting with local people to what to expect in its different regions.

This book will leave you with the inspiration, tools, and resources to make your Brazilian journey unlike any other.

And if you are not traveling to Brazil just yet, don't worry. These stories will entertain and inspire you. Remember, this is a whole new style of travel guide. Let the adventure begin.

Brazil

Brazil is the 5th largest country in the world. It's land mass is huge. We know it as the lungs of the world, home of the Amazon rainforest. Not to mention the biggest Carnival in the world, some of the world's most famous beaches, and Latin America's largest city. Brazil is a land of great contrasts. For many of us, Brazil provokes images of a samba soundtrack and waves crashing on the sand.

We also know Brazil as the host of the 2014 World Cup and the 2016 Olympics.

But this book is about more than that. It is about the inspiring stories of the people and places found all through this fascinating country and what we can learn from them.

This book will take you to the *favelas* and to the jungles; to the waterfalls and to the wetlands. It will show you a Brazil you never knew existed. One that is positive, inspiring, and incredible.

It will take you beyond Copacabana beach and Christ the Redeemer.

From the world's 5th largest country, we will hear stories from her heart and soul across all of her five regions.

About the Author

Before we hear the passionate, engaging stories of Brazil, let me introduce myself.

My name is Richard Brownsdon and I'm a travel writer, blogger, and journalist. I write about ecotourism, responsible travel, entrepreneurship, and social enterprise around the world.

I'm from the Isle of Man, a small but perfectly formed island between England and Ireland. My love of adventure comes from exploring this beautiful land, but that's another story.

I've written for international publications including The Guardian, Forbes, Virgin, Responsible Travel, and various inflight airline magazines. I'm also an international award winning blogger.

My work has been translated into Portuguese, Thai, and Japanese. I have travelled to more than 50 countries on six continents and I'm still going strong.

I love sharing the best of what I find with my readers. If you want to read other travel stories, or see the beautiful photos that accompany this book, you can find them at www. RichardBrownsdon.com

As well as travel and entrepreneurship writing, I also run a company called Inspiring Adventures. We provide top quality travel products that keep our customers happy and their valuables safe on their adventures.

Find out more and see our product range at www.Inspiring-Adventures.com. Get a 20% discount until December 31st, 2016 by using the promo code on the last page of this book.

And now, back to Brazil. Let's start with a little history.

A snapshot of Brazilian history

Brazil was colonized by the Portuguese in the 16th century and became a nation-state in 1822 when it declared its independence. Before that, many different Indigenous tribes made it their home. For a long time, it was believed that the rainforest was incapable of sustaining more than small and scattered populations; but the jungle holds many secrets. Recent archaeological discoveries instead point to a complex society which once covered the entire landmass. The Amazon rainforest may be the last place where there are still indigenous tribes unaffected by modern society.

The rainforest is also a place of extensive scientific research and environmental activity. The more we study it, the more we realize that we've barely scratched the surface. As recently as 2015, scientists had identified hundreds of previously unknown species including a purring monkey and a vegetarian piranha! And we also know that the Amazon rainforest is likely the largest repository of pharmaceuticals on the planet.

Yet, the Amazon is only one of the country's eco-regions. In the northeast and central areas, subsistence farming and agro-business compete in an inhospitable environment where the heat can be punishing. Vast tracts of forest have been cleared for cattle, corn, and soya bean farming. In the south, huge plantations grow cashew and sugar cane. Production of both crops can involve serious health risks for workers which is a constant struggle for producers looking to keep their costs down.

Then there's the *Pantanal*—shared with Bolivia and Paraguay— the world's largest tropical wetland and home to thousands of species of birds, fish, and reptiles, many of which are unique to the region. It also has large mammals such as marsh deer, jaguars, tapirs, and capybaras. This is the home of the legendary giant anaconda snake.

The industrial, highly urbanized south of Brazil is a more temperate zone. The equator crosses Brazil in the northeast though São Paulo, with its four seasons, is more than 2,500 km. further south.

With a population of 200 million, Brazil is by far the largest Portuguese-speaking country in the world and the only one in the western hemisphere. More than any other country in Latin America, Brazil was founded on slave labour. It's believed that some 4 million slaves were brought there from West Africa— almost twice the number of any other slave-trading nation— and Brazil was the last slave-trading nation to ban the practice in 1888.

During the Pangaean age some 300 million years ago, Brazil and West Africa fit together; although ever since the industrial age, they've been linked by a tragic slave history. This history has left a legacy of violence, poverty, racism, and social division which continue to cause issues today.

However, West Africans brought with them vibrant music, religion, dance, art, and food. This has added immeasurably to Brazil's culture. It's a glorious mélange. This is the true Brazil.

So, in this context of vibrancy, contrasts, and the strive to create a brighter future, let's visit the five regions of Brazil.

Part I: Five timeless truths from Brazil's guardians

1. Radical visions of hope
2. Just get started
3. Community rootedness
4. The power of mixing things up
5. Connecting from local to global and from traditional to modern

1. Radical visions of hope

Sometimes, in the midst of huge challenges, it's difficult to see where to go next or how to go forward at all. Brazil is a land of many contrasts; economic development and devastating environmental destruction; prosperity and socio-economic divisions; turbulent crime and an increasingly educated population. It takes true visionaries to imagine new futures.

These visionaries can be anywhere. Being locally based doesn't mean you can't dream up something big. Some people can just see potential where others cannot. This is a radical way of thinking which can lead to real change.

For me, Senhor Modesto Sampaio embodies this way of thinking. I arrived at the town of Bonito and began touring the eco projects in the area, among them, *Buraco Das Araras*. This is remarkable piece of land features the largest sinkhole in South

America and the second largest in the world. That may not sound so amazing in itself, but what Senhor Sampaio did with it was visionary.

The giant sandstone crater is more than 500 meters in circumference and 100 deep. At the bottom sits a green lake surrounded by lush forest. The crater is home to more than 130 bird species and all kinds of land creatures such as coati, anteaters, and armadillos. In the water, there are fish and even alligators. The place buzzes with life. But it wasn't always this way.

I met Senhor Sampaio after touring the area for a couple of days. He's a friendly, older gentleman; soft-spoken, compact, and sun-browned with a thicket of grey hair protruding under a large straw hat. He had a knowing twinkle in his eye.

He started telling me stories about the place. Before the mid-1980s, the crater was mainly used as a garbage pit and as a dumping ground for gangsters ridding themselves of unwanted evidence. Things were pretty grim and barren. Then, in the 1980s, the surrounding land—including the sinkhole—was purchased by a farmer who saw its potential.

Modest as his name, Senhor Modesto Sampaio didn't identify himself as the owner so it was a while before I realized I was speaking with the visionary himself. Farmers world-wide are known for being more practical than poetic so it wouldn't have been surprising if Senhor Sampaio had chosen to fill the sinkhole. That's what he had been advised to do by local engineers so he could use all the land for farming.

Instead, he put his charm and tenacity to work to convince the local fire brigade, a nearby university, and the military to help him remove truckloads of waste. A short time later, he was able to reintroduce wild, red-winged macaws which gave *Buraco das Araras*—Hole of the Macaws—its name. The hole has its own unique ecosystem. Now, more than 40 pairs of macaws live and breed in nooks in the crater walls and the amount and variety of wildlife is steadily increasing.

Senhor Sampaio and his sons have mostly stopped farming and are now able to rely entirely on the income that their sustainably managed tourism venture brings in. Tour group size is limited to 10 at a time and groups are always accompanied by a tour guide or local environmental monitor. The *Buraco Das Araras* website describes its tours as "*contemplative walks*." This is about much more than simply touring.

Thirty years ago, Senhor Sampaio saw potential where others saw only ruin; and now, the results of his vision are evident. In Senhor Sampaio's words, "We think it is rewarding work because if I were breeding cattle or planting crops, I'd have to deforest the land. But this way, I can protect the environment while giving work to local families."

You can see and hear some of the unique beauty of this place in the photos and videos on the *Buraco Das Araras* website (http://www.buracodasararas.tur.br/pt/).

Those who run the Santa Clara guesthouse in the *Pantanal* are similar in a way. They also saw the potential that was hidden from others.

Thirty years ago, the *Pantanal* was considered a backwater, chiefly notable for an infinite number of mosquitos and other annoying, disease ridden insects. It covers a vast river delta in the centre of the South American continent, spanning across large portions of Brazil, Bolivia, and Paraguay. It's the world's largest tropical wetlands and it is full of intrigue.

Even its exact size isn't known. Estimates range from 54—75,000 square kilometres. It is of hydrodynamic importance to the entire continent and is now recognized as a UNESCO World Heritage site. It's estimated that the *Pantanal* is home to more than 1,000 species of birds, 400 of fish, nearly 500 of reptiles, 300 of mammals, and countless others of different families. But no one really knows for sure.

So are all these creatures dangerous? Not at all! They include the unassuming tapir, the gorgeous hyacinth macaw, comical capybaras, howler monkeys, the giant river otter, wary marsh deer, and the elusive jaguar. However, given that the *Pantanal* is largely swampland, there are a lot of biting insects as well as many we normally want to stay away from—for example, things with very sharp teeth like caymans and piranhas. Yet here, too, visionaries have seen potential. Slowly but surely, a unique brand of down-and-dirty adventurous eco-tourism has started to grow.

I was able to experience this first hand from the Santa Clara guesthouse (http://www.pantanalsantaclara.com.br/pagina-inicial.html). Upon arrival, I was greeted by a friendly macaw. All around us were giant hyacinth macaws—the largest of the species—along with *hundreds* of birds from dozens of species that flew throughout the grounds. Another macaw welcomed me at the check-in desk. Hawks patrolled the garden. Parakeets zipped along in pairs. A toucan watched from a distance.

Piranha fishing was on offer so I didn't hesitate on signing up. We were a group of four: Udo and Gisele—a German couple—myself, and Alex, our energetic guide. We were to fish, not from some boring dock or boat, but from the side of an extremely muddy, steep-sloped riverbank! Alex advised us to take off our shoes to give ourselves a better grip. But mightn't our gripping toes also be attractive to caymans lurking in the water? Sure enough, it wasn't long before one showed up with an undue interest in our toes!

We fought him off by hitting him with our fishing rods as if whacking cayman was the most natural thing to do. With the cayman watching from a distance, we attached our bait and cast a line. It took about three seconds to get a bite from a hungry piranha—less time than it took to get the bait on the hook. In this river, the water was too muddy to see through but it just had to be *full* of piranha...

We weren't just fishing—we were sliding slowly through the mud into the piranha-infested waters on the sides of a slippery riverbank while fighting off cayman and trying not to be eaten alive by mosquitos.

Do you think that sounds like something tourists would want to do?

Well, someone with vision *did* and I was able to have a great adventure as a result. But much more importantly, this area is better protected than ever because of the care taken by the guides, the ecological awareness raised with the tourists, and the generated income which finances much needed conservational programmes.

At the end of the day, back at the guesthouse we grilled and ate our piranhas while celebrating not being eaten by anything ourselves—except for the mosquitos!

2. Just get started

Brazil's guardians taught me that sometimes the time to do something is *now*. You just have to get started—without a grand plan, without really knowing what you're doing, but just knowing that you need to do *something* and following that instinct.

Luti Guedes is a youthful and inspiring example. Talking to Luti (pronounced *Loo-chee*) is an experience in enthusiasm. He's thin, not too tall, and has a very expressive, be-spectacled face which shines with delight when he talks about his projects.

When Luti was 16, he travelled to Marajo Island in the northern Amazonas state and it changed his life. He saw people in rural communities living without clean water, electricity, schools, or hospitals—things which he considered basic necessities. He wishes they could have the same privileges he enjoyed.

Maybe if he'd been older and wiser, he'd have approached things differently; but he was 16 and full of passion. He started an organization called *Lute Sem Fronteiras*—Struggle Without Borders. The word "struggle" here is a play on his own name which is pronounced the same way. It creates the impression that he, himself, knows no boundaries. *Lute Sem Fronteiras* has brought libraries, agricultural education, micro-finance, and schools to rural Amazonas communities.

"Nobody would say that I could do this at 16, 17, or 18 years old—but I have!" Luti says with a disarming sense of disbelief. When I ask how he did it...well, he says, he just jumped in and got started! The first need he saw was for books. So, why not build a library? He started by raising funds from friends and family, and then friends of friends. He just kept at it until he had raised enough. Then the next project came up, and the next, and the next.

One of Luti's favourite aspects of how *Lute Sem Fronteiras* runs is its do-one/give-one principle. When a project begins—like building a library or establishing an agricultural education course—the community is involved but they benefit from outside resources. Though once their project is up and running, it's up to the community to start another one somewhere else. This way, change multiplies.

Luti quickly started forming partnerships and presenting his work at different events. He was still just in his early 20s and a fulltime law student when I met him and he's been learning as he goes. He continues to make useful connections with entrepreneurs who are mentoring him and encouraging him to think even bigger.

"If you're waiting for someone to tell you that you can do something, you'll be waiting all your life," he says. "Don't wait for someone to tell you that you can do something like this. Just start. I did, and now it's really helping people."

Luti: funny and lively, open and energetic, hard-working and a *starter*.

Another inspiring starter I know is Carmel Croukamp, the daughter of the founders of the *Parque das Aves*, a bird park near Iguaçu falls (http://www.parquedasaves.com.br/en/). Carmel Says:

"One of the most interesting concepts from the *Parque das Aves* story is that, when starting your own enterprise, it's never possible to correctly assess all the risks or the possibility of success. Successful enterprise is just about starting something and then going all out, fighting to the death and developing your product as you go along."

She jokes: "Most people are far too sensible to start their own business."

Today, Parque das Aves sits right next to the Iguaçu National Park. This thriving social and conservation project is visited by tens of thousands of tourists every year. The park allows people to experience close contact with native jungle birds and its entry fees support breeding programmes for endangered species, reintroduction programmes, scientific research, education, and more. But getting to this stage was pretty tough.

The story goes back to the 1970s when Dennis and Anna Croukamp, an entrepreneur and a vet respectively, were given a bald, ugly baby African Grey parrot which they hand raised. He became a member of the family, flying free outside during the day, eating at the dinner table, and then drifting to sleep under a tea towel on Dennis' lap every evening.

Dennis and Anna fell in love with parrots. Eventually, they amassed quite a collection of them.

When they retired on the Isle of Man, Dennis got very bored. One day, a former business partner visited and told Dennis about a place in Brazil with the most beautiful waterfalls and that he thought they should build a crocodile farm there together. Dennis replied, "I don't like crocodiles; I like birds."

So, birds it was. Initially, the idea was to put together a project proposal and raise capital from large investors. However, in those days the Brazilian currency was in hyperinflation and rule of law, only a few years after the collapse of a military dictatorship, was fairly sparse. The Ernst and Young handbook on how to do business in Brazil simply said: "Don't."

Almost inevitably, their investment deals fell through. Dennis lost his business partner and he was left with the decision of losing all the capital he'd invested so far or of going all in and risking his whole retirement fund to finance it himself. Dennis was passionate about this project. He decided to risk everything.

He spoke no Portuguese and he knew nothing about building a zoo or tourism. All this in a climate that was fundamentally uninviting to entrepreneurship. But he and Anna poured in all their money, eventually selling their cars[1], jewellery, and

---

[1] On an interesting personal side note, when I was 13 my dad bought one of the cars which helped to finance the park. Read the story at www.RichardBrownsdon.com/?s=bird

everything of value. This enabled them to start building. When they ran out of money, they opened the park to a small trickle of visitors.

Then, Dennis died.

Anna was all in. She had never run a business but she picked up everything and moved to Brazil. As with so many important steps in life, she says that had she known in advance all the obstacles she would face, she'd have been too terrified to go through with it.

For years, it seemed everything was working against her. Everyone from shady businessmen to government officials tried to get the park closed down. But her perseverance paid off and Anna quickly became a shrewd entrepreneur. Over the years she was able to attract more and more business partners. Somewhere during these difficult times, Anna's daughter Carmel decided to change her life path—slated for Oxford studying music—and also moved to Brazil to carry on her father's dream. "When would a chance like that ever come up again?" she said. She too, jumped right in.

Now, *Parque das Aves* is the biggest bird park in Latin America and sees over 500,000 visitors each year. And it all started with just getting started.

3. Community rootedness

I quickly began to see how important it is for projects to be rooted in the communities where they are located. Of course, I already knew this, but experiencing it first hand was something different.

Fight for Peace (http://fightforpeace.net) shows this in spades. This project, in the Maré *favela* of Rio de Janeiro, seeks to inspire young people by teaching them boxing and martial arts. The academy has grown from helping 10 disadvantaged youth in 2000 when it was formed to serving more than 2,500 *each year*.

Luke, the founder, is passionate about the community and helping the kids who live there. In fact, he has committed his life to this cause. He's now an award-winning social entrepreneur and Ashoka fellow (https://www.ashoka.org).

In keeping with Luke's vision, *Fight for Peace* isn't just a boxing academy. It provides high school education and, just as importantly, a sense of belonging and meaning. It gives kids something positive to fight for. The brand has become so strong in the *favela* that people steal *Fight for Peace* t-shirts from washing lines just because they want to be associated with it. The project has now gone global.

Bela Arte Jazz is a similar kind of project located in Cantagalo, another Rio *favela*. Learning jazz music might seem worlds away from boxing and martial arts but this community rooted project also gives young people something to strive.

Bela Arte Jazz was started by Leonardo Januario, a free-lance musician and Cantagalo resident. As a community member, he's not only helping others but fulfilling his own dream to create the first *favela* big jazz band and, "to be able to wander around *Cantagalo* while hearing the sounds of jazz echoing through the neighbourhood."

He collects instruments, which he loans out to students, and runs his jazz classes for free. Performance events are also often free and sell snacks and drinks in order to raise funds for the school.

These projects are intentionally setting out to create change—especially among the youth. But even projects which seem to have nothing at all to do with social change can have an impact on the communities where they're located. Being rooted enables them to be a force for positive change.

Flavio Hauser exemplifies this. He has a smiling face and very short-cropped hair which recedes a little and is just starting to turn grey. When he talks about the many innovations his business has adopted, his eyes light up. He's in his early 40s, married with young children, and happy with his life and the community where he lives. There's a sense of purposeful, unhurried peace about him.

His mother had a dream of setting up a resort in Brazil but never had the chance to do it. But he could. He and his business partner established *Lagoa do Cassange* as an eco-resort and have been developing it, little-by-little, for the past 20 years. It's simple, beautiful, and important to Flavio, partly because of his mother's dreams from long-ago.

But the community is important to him too and he wants to see it thrive. That is why he's been building his resort in a way that also builds his community. First and foremost, *Lagoa do Cassange* (http://www.lagoadocassange.com.br) uses sustainable practices like solar power, recycling, composting, re-greening, rainwater collection, alternative building materials, and sourcing local products wherever possible.

But it goes much further than this. *Lagoa do Cassange* runs free adult education courses, built a kindergarten school, teaches leadership skills, and runs computer classes for more than 100 residents. They teach environmental awareness through beach clean-up days and they run a honey project through which, in exchange for training to produce honey and the income from selling it, families commit to maintaining and preserving their patch of rainforest.

Why does a business do all this? Well, there's a practical aspect as well. The resort needs trained adults so offering free training means better workforce options and a greater likelihood that, rather than going to the big cities for work, those with potential will stay in the community. Schooling for children supports the workforce by making it more attractive for young families to stay and contribute. Everyone benefits from a healthy community. They team up with other resorts and encourage them to do the same in order to spread the impact.

EcoPousada Miriti (*pousada* means *inn*) (http://www. miritipousada.com.br), run by Geraldo and Pricila Barata, takes a very similar approach. It's a tranquil guesthouse located in Belem, a northern port city in the state of Pará. It has been lovingly designed with sustainable values right in the heart of the city.

EcoPousada Miriti is eco in many ways. Its water filtration system cleans out 70% of the chemicals before it's returned to the water table where natural processes do the rest (most guesthouses in Brazil don't filter water at all). Solar power heats the water and the system will have paid for itself in six years. But how did it all get started?

Pricila was a tourism student who wrote her final dissertation on sustainable guesthouses. Based on this work, she and Geraldo wrote what would become the business plan for *EcoPousada Miriti*. Pricila's mother had purchased a property in need of renovation and the pair set about transforming it.

Demolishing the old buildings and starting anew would have been the easy, obvious choice. But they chose to renovate instead. There were many good reasons why. If you demolish, the waste has to go somewhere—and that means adding to landfill. Then, building anew means buying and using more materials, more resources. Renovation means you spend less on materials, but more on labour. Pricila and Geraldo, apart from reducing their ecological footprint, preferred to invest in local labour over new materials. Any new materials they did need were sourced locally.

And they didn't stop there. *EcoPousada Miriti* supports local artisans to create toys from the leaves of the Miriti Palm—from which the guesthouse takes its name. These toys have a long tradition but without a place like *EcoPousada Miriti* they would never be sold and the traditional skills needed to make them would be lost.

I was inspired by these and other examples of the power of being rooted right into the community: engaging community members, listening to them, and taking advantage of their expertise, creativity, and resourcefulness.

In the end, it has to do with respecting that you are part of a community and remembering that you can do more together.

4. The power of mixing things up

Some of the projects I visited seemed to have developed in bits with new parts added on as opportunity and inspiration arose. This resulted in lovely, idiosyncratic combinations such as traditional toy-making alongside eco-construction or computer training next to a kindergarten and guesthouse, as in the examples shared in the previous chapter. But I learned that mixing missions into sometimes whimsical pairings could also be quite powerful.

Without a doubt, one of the most enjoyable was *The Queen* nail bar in Campo Grande. Was this "nail" as in manicures? And "bar" as in drinks? Well, yes it was. An odd combination indeed, but why *The Queen*? Because the owner, a beautiful young woman called Bia Figueiredo, had spent three years living in London and loved all things British. Her salon was full of British memorabilia and knick-knacks such as the famous "keep calm" sign and even a red telephone box. Wherever did she get those?

In fact, Bia had reached out to invite me to her salon, purely because she had heard someone from London was visiting her town and she wanted to offer her hospitality.

Nail bars aren't normally on the Inspiring Adventures tour map—but since this was, after all, all about adventure, I opted to spend the afternoon on a kind of blind spa date. It went something like this:

Bia treated me to a caipiroska, or was it a caipirinha? I can't remember; we shared drinks anyway. *She really knows how to put the bar in Nail Bar*. We chatted about London while one of her staff spiffed up my nails. Then, we moved to the outside area where the three of us shared a mojito fishbowl. This is one of Bia's favourites drinks from a bar called Casa Blue on Bricklane in London which she'd lovingly. Because Bia and her friend were both driving, most of the drinking was left up to me. No problem.

Even though I was now a bit drunk, Bia was polite enough to invite me to watch her friends play water volleyball in a private pool nearby. Not an everyday activity in the UK. We watched, drank, and then began to feel hungry. So what would any good Londoner do? I treated Bia to a local kebab! After a quick drive around town, Bia drove me back to my guesthouse. What a quirky, wonderful afternoon!

And powerful in an unexpected way. That mishmash of elements created something unique and unforgettable while giving me a top-notch experience of Brazilian hospitality.

But this is only the tip of the iceberg, or Sugar Loaf, as the case may be. Mixing things up turned out to be inspiring and life-changing as well. Just think of *Fight for Peace* using boxing or *Cantagalo* using the cool sounds of jazz to address underdevelopment, youth disaffection, violence, and unemployment. There's no straight line from martial arts or jazz to community development; but it is working.

Another example is agro-eco-tourism; a mash-up of three different sectors. What is this exactly? And how do they all fit together?

I learned about this at the San Francisco Lodge (http://www. fazendasanfrancisco.tur.br) in the *Pantanal* from its owner Roberto Coelho. "Agro," he explained, "because we teach people about farming. Eco, because we introduce people to our unique wildlife and nature." And tourism, obviously, because they welcome people like me from all over the world.

San Francisco Lodge sits on a 15,000 hectare property which Roberto inherited from his father. It has been farmed for many years, principally for cattle and rice. Roberto wanted to develop the farm with the latest technology such as specialized breeding. But he also loved the rich diversity of the land, including the flooded parts where the interspersed areas of irrigation and tillage attracted a wide variety of animals. Developing eco-tourism meant increasing the operation's income which, importantly, made it profitable to preserve the rich biological diversity of the land. The San Francisco homestead no longer had to bow to the relentless pressures of agribusiness. Eight thousand of the 15,000 hectares remain as natural reserve and according to Roberto, "will always stay that way!"

Just as importantly, Roberto explains the social impact of this mixed approach. "As a small example," he says, "the men of the local families work on the farm and their wives, who are not trained in farming skills, are still able to work with the tourists— for example, in the kitchen cooking delicious food."

Like Flavio Hauser, Roberto recognizes the importance of a happy workforce. San Francisco Lodge ran a free bus for 15 years so that local children could get to school in the nearest city. Now that there's a public bus service, San Francisco's educational support has not ended. They provide adult education classes to all staff on subjects like health and safety, first aid, and food hygiene. Teens and young adults of employees' families are invited to attend as well—thus investing in the operation's future workforce and the future of the greater community.

At San Francisco, you can see thousands of birds—from giant storks to jewel-like kingfishers; from pink spoonbills to dark, circling hawks and foraging woodpeckers. The *Pantanal* is a stopping place and wintering ground for three of the world's great migratory flyways. Ospreys from Arctic latitudes far to the north, wood storks from the pampas to the south, and flycatchers from the Andes to the west.

Capybaras are out in numbers and if you're lucky you might also see tapirs, monkeys, anteaters—and on night safaris, tawny ocelots.

San Francisco, *Fight for Peace*, *Cantagalo Jazz*, and even *The Queen* all taught me in new ways about how, when you're willing to mix things up a bit, the whole can be much greater than the sum of its beautiful parts!

5. Connecting from local to global and from traditional to modern.

Brazil may have some of the world's best examples of how the modern and the traditional, and the local and the global can go hand-in-hand, each one complementing the other. Here, a damp patch of rainforest is not so far removed from international markets. *100% Amazonia* (http://theamazinamazon.com/) is an inspiring example of how this works.

Part of their mission is to "...transform isolated communities into citizens of a sustainable global culture." Co-founder, Fernanda Stefani, describes *100% Amazonia* as a solution provider—a matchmaker of sorts between local resources and traditional knowledge here and the vast global marketplace out there. At *100% Amazonia's* headquarters, I passed barrels of fruit pulp ready to be shipped to China and açaí roots prepared for shipping to the United States. The warehouse was packed with seeds, oils, salves, and some cool items called *bio-jewellery*.

I was treated to a cup of thick, rich açaí juice—some of the finest I'd tasted. The international market has really opened up for açaí. In the UK, *100% Amazonia* already supplies Mangajo and has developed beers based on Amazonian ingredients.

The Amazon is rich in vegetation that can be sustainably harvested and rich in local knowledge on the versatility of its vast quantity of produce. Harvesting, rather than farming, means that products grow naturally and there's no deforestation with its well-known, disastrous results. These operations are small footprint.

But how can local people get their products to market? International shipping logistics and documentation is, as Fernanda explains, quite complex and negotiating with large companies is difficult for individuals.

For these reasons, *100% Amazonia* instead connects local harvesters with international distributors. It provides fair prices to indigenous people, helps them collaborate to get the best deals, and then operates all the international trade logistics.

And it really does prove that what's good for local communities and good for the planet can be good for business as well. *100% Amazonia*'s revenue has doubled every year since 2009.

Ethical, globally-connected enterprises like this are becoming more common and *Preserva Mundi* (www.preservamundi.com. br/) is just another example. It focuses mainly on neem, noni, and andiroba; three plant-based super products which can be made into a vast range of products. Neem, in particular, has many applications. These include natural pesticides, vermicides, fungicides, insect repellent, salves, toothpaste, teas, juices, oils, and much more. *Preserva Mundi's* mission is *"to end the use of poisons in the world."*

In agriculture, when neem is left growing in pastures, cattle ingest a small amount of it. This aids their digestion and helps them fight disease. It also cuts down on the insect population in their dung and has been proven to help plant roots grow thicker and stronger.

These are things the world wants and companies like *Preserva Mundi* are creating the link between local producers and the global marketplace in thoughtful, sustainable ways.

I was given some neem samples of oil, mosquito repellent, and soap. This turned out to be very lucky for me because my next stop was the Brazilian wetlands, in the wet season, surrounded by water, and just after the rain—Mosquito heaven. I put on the repellent every day and it worked a treat for me. It was great to have a natural product that I could cover myself in without feeling like a toxic chemical dump. Thank you neem and *Preserva Mundi*!

And thank you solution providers who have enabled us to benefit from the rainforest's incredible bounty.

Thinking back and looking forward

Thinking back, I realize that these five timeless truths from which I learned so much from Brazil's guardians are not unconnected. It seems to me that there's a kind of trajectory running through them. Vision is the first thing. You can't accomplish anything without it. **Radical visions of hope**, such as the ones I saw, are even more awe inspiring.

But then you have to jump in; **just get started** somehow. Here, **community rootedness** becomes critical. You can't make much headway—and certainly not sustainable progress—without it.

Working with communities means you now get all kinds of perspectives you didn't have before and your opportunities for **mixing things up** in new, fun, and ultimately productive ways just keep on expanding.

From there, if you're lucky and intentional, you can **connect the dots between the local and the global, the traditional and the tech-savvy**, in positive ways. None of us is an island. John Donne said that way back in the 16th century and we've always known it; but today we *experience* it, every day, to be acutely true.

Upon leaving Brazil and so many wonderful people of good faith whom I'd been privileged to meet, I felt myself to be within a complex, evolving, brilliant, and often challenging web of relationships and interconnections. I felt fortunate enough to have been woven in.

This is why we need responsible, thoughtful ways to be together. Responsible, inspiring business and travel. And this is why I wrote part 2: Five steps to eco-travel success in Brazil.

Part 2: Five steps to eco-travel success in Brazil

1. Connect with local entrepreneurs and change makers.

2. Challenge your assumptions and be ready to be surprised.

3. Travel to different regions—they're all vastly different.

4. Accept unexpected hospitality and open up to new experiences.

5. Revere and revel in nature.

1. Connect with local entrepreneurs and change makers

It goes without saying that travel experiences are vastly enhanced by connecting with locals. There are many ways to do this, but for a modern day eco tourist, none is better than connecting with local change makers. I was fortunate to get to know so many amazing entrepreneurs who rewarded me with experiences and insights that I'd otherwise never have known about: Luti, Senhor Sampaio, Fernanda, and the others whose stories are chronicled in part 1.

It's worth taking a somewhat systematic approach. As I have promoted eco-tourism on my website, I was able to connect with eco-entrepreneurs across the country to profile them and tell their stories. This made it easy for them to say "yes" to my visit and it also added layers of richness and discovery to my travels through the simple act of meeting local people.

Whatever your business or talent, chances are there are others like you out there who will be happy to meet up and show you around.

For the travelling entrepreneur, a trip to a local co-working space can be a great way to meet local entrepreneurs. I visited the Experimental.cc co-working space in Rio de Janeiro (http://experimental.cc) and Impact Hub São Paulo (http://saopaulo.impacthub.com.br). These are trendy, cool places (they even have swimming pools) that attract the talented and entrepreneurial.

Here, like in any co-working hub, change-makers get access to bright open space, high-speed internet, office supplies to run their businesses, and other amenities which can vary from place to place (did I mention swimming pools?). But more importantly, like in any good co-working space, people can rub shoulders with each other, attend social and learning events, exchange ideas, and reach across sectors and disciplines to create new and innovate things. It's an ideal kind of place for engaged entrepreneurs to meet likeminded individuals.

One of the first people I contacted was Ilya Brotsky, a Canadian living the start-up life in Rio. He invited me round to his co-working space and start-up incubator called 21212 (http://21212.com/) which builds entrepreneurial capacity through online resources and peer learning. I wasn't really surprised to find him and his team still working when I got there at 7 p.m. They'd recently secured investment, had had some big coverage, and the new website was about to go live. As usual, last minute changes were quickly being put into place.

During dinner and while waiting for a bus, Ilya and I discussed the struggles of start-up life and how lucky we are to spend our time doing things we feel passionately about. There's no certainty in our future but at least, for the moment, we're in control of our direction and we like where it's heading.

I met up with Ilya and his team again the next night for a samba class at the appropriately named Gringo Cafe. After samba, we were ready for Carnival. We followed the music-playing trucks and quickly became surrounded by hordes of drummers. One member of the team, Olivia, introduced me to the sweet delicacies of Brazil, like the *brigaderio*, a sweet chocolate truffle. After a little more dancing we headed to Ipanema beach where we couldn't help noticing all the drunk Carnival couples making out. An entrepreneurial visit had turned into an amazing social occasion with a front-row local's view of one of the world's great spectacles!

My meeting the next day was a completely different experience. A man named Severino had sent me a message through an online entrepreneurial website saying he'd like to meet me and was interested in business for social benefit. I got the sense he was using Google Translate. Years of teaching English in Japan had taught me the difference between a computer translator and not-so-great English.

I was right. Severino could speak no English and I no Portuguese. At his office, we tried valiantly to communicate using single words of each other's language. After 10 minutes of good-hearted struggle, we turned on the computer, loaded Google Translate, and got down to business. It worked surprisingly well.

We discussed the struggles of life in Brazil, politics, corruption, social enterprise, our motivations, and travels. I really appreciated his interest in my work and he thanked me for coming to Brazil to share positive stories from social entrepreneurs. He told me he was inspired to do more and will free up some time to hire out his office free of charge to socially responsible entrepreneurs. It was pretty rewarding to potentially plant seeds of future social action and connect Severino with some of the right people to get started.

At the Impact Hub co-working space in São Paulo, I had a different experience. I met Pedro Vitoriano who was planning an epic trip to visit social entrepreneurs in not just all five regions, but in all 27 states of Brazil (http://www.projetobrasil27.com.br). A graduate of Cambridge University and independent researcher at one of Brazil's top universities, Pedro works in and extensively studies Brazil's social enterprise sector.

I spent a fun day working at Impact Hub which included being treated to a typical fried lunch with Pedro.

His journey chronicle is now a treasure trove of information for anyone wanting to connect with social entrepreneurs in Brazil. If you don't read Portuguese, you can use your browser's *translate page* function to read the case studies Pedro has documented.

Let the connecting-across-borders begin!

2. Challenge your assumptions and be ready to be surprised.

Good travel always includes a healthy dose of challenging your assumptions. Sometimes we don't even know our assumptions are there until they are confronted. Here's an example.

I mentioned my visit to Carnival with my new friends in Rio. It wasn't by accident I'd arrived in Brazil at that time. Carnival in Rio is legendary! Something like a million people come to celebrate the monumental event. It was overwhelming at times but the official Carnival parade didn't wholly meet the assumptions I didn't even know I'd had.

While most activities happen freely on the streets with people young and old following music blaring trucks, the parade is the real attraction—dubbed the *Greatest Show on Earth*. Though it was amazing, I wouldn't say it was the greatest on Earth. I found myself, perhaps unfairly, comparing it to Olympic opening and closing ceremonies. It's on that scale but it's not same. It's about eight hours (!) of hordes of people in bright costumes parading along the Sambadrome (a custom walkway with spectator seats on either side).

There weren't quite as many women in skimpy outfits as I'd been led to believe from all the marketing. There were, however, *thousands* of people with enormous amounts of colourful plastic stuck to them. It had everything from human snakes with footballs in their mouths (I don't know why), to scuba divers, to ... a kind of human oil slick? Hard to explain; weird to see. Only a few of the floats really amazed me, like the one with some kind of giant animatronic Neanderthals or the one with a huge glowing lizard with free-floating jelly-fish.

The *favelas* of Rio challenged my assumptions in a different way. For an eye-opening experience, taking an ethical *favela* tour is high on my recommended list of activities. I wasn't sure if I should even take my camera or if I had to keep it in my bag the whole time.

In fact, that was one of the first things I asked my guide, Gabriel. Maybe you have heard how dangerous the *favelas* can be and I believe some of them are. But with expert local guidance they're as safe as the streets in any other city.

Just like in London, there are neighbourhoods where you can go and places you shouldn't. Having a local to help you tell the difference is essential.

Cantagalo, a *favela* I visited just off Copacabana beach used to be a haven for drug gangs, dealers, and criminals. Definitely not a safe place for a tourist or even a city local. However, many of these communities are undergoing rapid development. Change is in the air through a mixture of government pacification of criminal gangs, urban development, and upcoming social projects. Some of the most inspiring people I met lived right there in the *favelas*, working with their communities on unique, life-giving ventures.

On the other hand, who would have thought that fishing on a mosquito infested riverbank into piranha and crocodile infested waters would have been so much fun or that being willing to take the un-macho step of having a manicure would lead to a super fun afternoon around town with a local Brit enthusiast

Travel is always full of surprises; but allowing our assumptions and openness to be challenged will add to the experience immeasurably—especially in a place of such extremes and contrasts as Brazil.

3. Travel to different regions—they're all vastly different.

From afar, it's difficult to realize just how big and diverse Brazil really is. Maps typically show vast swaths of dense green representing the Amazon rainforest and the ever so long snake of the Amazon River—but there's much more to Brazil than that. Brazil spans four time zones and shares a border with every South American country except Chile and Ecuador. It has

17 cities with a population of over a million and more than 4,000 airports. The environment is Caribbean in the northeast, dense tropical rainforest in the north and interior, vast swamplands in the centre south, and temperate with distinct seasons in the south.

Some areas have very large populations of West African descendants and retain many African cultural influences, some are mixed, and others are dominated by those of Western European descent. You can't just visit one corner and say you've seen Brazil!

I set out from the beginning to visit all five regions of Brazil and I'm glad I did. Here's why.

Central region: This is the location of the amazing *Pantanal* and where you'll find some of the best eco-tourism around. Here, I was welcomed by local expert, photographer, journalist, and author Fabio Pellegrini. I'd just taken an overnight flight and Fabio met me at the airport. We spent the day planning my stay in the region and discussing must-see sights and eco-tourism activities. Fabio knows everyone and is the go-to person in the *Pantanal* area. When you plan your trip, get in touch with him! (http://fabiopellegrini.com.br).

Fabio helped me connect with unique venues like *Buraco Das Araras* and creative approaches like the agro-eco-tourism of San Francisco Lodge—both visited in part 1. He'll help you jump into some very unique activities such as piranha fishing, also recounted earlier.

Another example is *Bonito*, the epicentre of responsible travel and ecotourism in Brazil. One of the leading responsible tourism operators there is *Ygarape* (http://www.ygarape.com.br). It's founder, Juca Ygarape, really came across as the father of eco-tourism in the area. He discovered many of *Bonito's* local attractions and he's the man Discovery Channel or National

Geographic call when they need a local expert. Juca showed me a video of him tracking a huge anaconda in the water and introducing it to scientists and professional photojournalists.

Over the years, Juca and his friends have been responsible for designing many of the guiding principles that ensure the sustainability of Bonito's tourist trade. For example, Bonito is famous for its rivers of crystal clear water, some of which have an underwater visibility of up to 40 metres! There's now a limit on the number and group size of daily visitors. Snorkelers are reminded not to touch the riverbed or even to use sunscreen or insect repellent because it disturbs the natural environment. These steps to preserve the natural environment while opening it up to tourism are paying off with a thriving industry.

I joined a snorkelling tour of Rio Da Pratawith with a group of about 12 people. We started with a short guided jungle walk (in our wetsuits!) and arrived at a fish filled lagoon of about 100 metres in diameter. Once in the water, you become accustomed to seeing large *pacus* (a piranha relative without the pointed teeth) or huge, carnivorous *dourados* ominously following you around. There are dozens of species of small fish here too— some of which like to nibble on your dead skin. Something I'd never seen before were the underground water sources that bubbled up on the riverbed like a strange, sandy soup.

In Bonito, I also took a boat ride down Rio Formoso. We were in a kind of white water raft although Formoso is actually pretty calm. There were a few little waterfalls to go over with a nice swimming spot at the end. Scuba diving in the river was challenging and fun. In the capable hands of scuba instructor Benicio Silveira, we dived down and even passed under a small waterfall. For some reason, a couple of giant, tame *dourado* fish followed us along the way. They felt a bit like guard dogs patrolling the water. One of my favourite moments was when

I popped up and surprised another group of tourists who were happily floating overhead on rubber rings – I felt a bit like I was in the Special Forces but without all the guns.

And then there's the *Gruta do Lago Azul*—the mysterious, luminous blue waters of an underground cave. Once again, tourist numbers here are strictly limited and monitored. The beautiful cave houses an unusually clear, blue lake. Apparently, tourists used to swim there but these days the waters are protected from us dirty human swimmers.

These are only a few examples of the stellar eco-tours you can experience in the Central region.

Northeast region: If there's one word to describe the Northeast; it's vibrant. It boasts some of the world's most beautiful beaches, a laid-back vibe, and colourful, African-influenced music and culture. Here, you'll find a rich history, delicious food, and a sustainable tourism scene—like *Lagoa do Cassange* featured in part 1.

The Northeast is home to Salvador; a city and experience not to be missed. I stayed at a place from AirBnB and Gerald, my wonderful host, was very welcoming. His house was large and he spoke some English. I had a single bed in what used to be his daughter's room, judging by the My Little Pony stickers on the cupboards.

I'd planned to meet a friend for dinner but when that didn't work out Gerald already had a plan B. He offered to take me to the last night of Carnival himself! So we hopped on his motorbike and rode 30 minutes to the centre of the Old Town.

I'm very fortunate that I got to experience a slightly more traditional carnival in the North of Brazil in addition that of Rio. Besides the marching drumming bands, the costumes, music, and dance had a strong African influence which was an interesting contrast to the heavily ornamented, plastic costumes of Rio. Of course, there were also the trucks blasting out live music from some of Brazil's most popular bands. I'd heard that Fatboy Slim and Gangnam Style were playing in Salvador although I wasn't in the right place to see either of them that night. Instead, I had an excellent time with Gerald, his cousin, and a fun motorbike ride each way.

It was my experience with Gerald that inspired my company's first travel product – a money belt. Although Carnival is generally safe, Gerald knew I looked like a tourist and would be an easy target for local pickpockets. He insisted I keep my valuables safe by shoving them into my underpants!

Luckily, I had a money belt with me. I was able to carry my phone and cash in secret under my clothes without having to use my underwear. My company, www.Inspiring-Adventures.com, now offers money belts, neck wallets, and more to travellers as I know firsthand how important it is to keep your valuables safe when travelling.

North region: The north boasts the most impressive botanical and biological wonders of the Amazon and some of the most interesting sustainable eco-enterprises in the country.

Some of these make ample use of traditional and local practices alongside technological advances. Even though they are very much locally rooted, products from this region are sold all over the world. This mix of local and global; old and new; makes a visit to the north a rich learning experience.

One of my favourite activities was a one-day boat tour and jungle walk courtesy of Amazon Star Tour Operators (http://amazonstar.com.br).

Our jovial guide for the day was Edilson. He explained we would be sailing past *Hiberinos*; or river people. These are not indigenous tribes but groups of creoles (Brazilians of mixed-African descent). Many are subsistence farmers and fishermen although some work in tourism.

We stopped on one island and Edlison introduced us to a variety of jungle wildlife. He named more varieties of fruit than I could write down or remember. We tried freshly gathered Brazil nuts, cacao fruit, and saw the famous açaí tree.

One local in his 80s demonstrated both his fitness and the difficulty of harvesting açaí berries. He climbed five metres up a tree and then jumped over to the next one to collect a few more berries! This was rewarded with an appreciative round of applause.

We had a little time to catch a tarantula and say hello to a parrot before heading back to the boat where we enjoyed lunch—and a storm. Rain pelted us on the way back and the roads flooded. This is the Amazon *rain* forest, after all.

Southeast region: In the southeast are the famous beaches and the sights of Rio as well as its *favelas*, some of which turned out to be very up-and-coming. This is also the country's industrial and commercial heartland and home to many of the nation's top universities. Here, you will find the country's most famous tourist destinations and hear some cool *Bossa Nova* sounds. You can also expect to find co-working hubs and lively entrepreneurism.

Don't be afraid to talk to people! On my short flight from São Paulo to Rio, I met a lovely student called Eleana. After we landed, she offered to show me around the sights and sounds of Carnival. Now I could explore the city with a new local friend.

Of course, it's important to be outgoing and positive on your travels. By smiling and being open, you'll easily attract these kinds of people in friendly, outgoing Brazil.

I met wonderful people in all of Brazil's regions—on planes, on buses, at parties, and sometimes through websites like CouchSurfing (couchsurfing.com).

South region: My predominant impressions of the south were its natural wonders. Iguaçu Falls and the surrounding area is not to be missed. As we learned in part 1 with the story of *Parque das Aves*, it's also the scene of some pretty amazing social enterprise and education.

It's clear that a big part of the *Parque*'s success is down to the amazing staff they employ. Juliana Ebling, the Environmental Education Coordinator, is also president of the Brazilian Environmental Educators Association and is affiliated with government policy makers.

Juliana and Carmel explained that the city of Foz do Iguaçu, where the bird park and Iguaçu Falls are located, has been through huge change in recent decades. In the 1970s, the construction of the Itaipu Dam and the hydro-electric plant was one of the largest construction projects in the world. It still remains the largest hydro-electric plant in terms of power output. The project brought workers from around the world and the population in Foz shot up from 20,000 to 120,000.

When construction ended 10 years later, there weren't enough local jobs to go around. Smuggling, poaching, and unscrupulous tourism operating became popular career choices. But Juliana had always pushed for change and it's starting to take effect.

After two years of trying to teach in universities, Juliana was invited to give lectures on conservation and environmental education to students studying at the Foz College for Tour Guides.

Her lectures focused on the importance of education while guiding. "When young environmental educators take their learning to more people and to other parts of Brazil, that's when we see attitudes towards the environment change on a large scale. That's the most rewarding part of the work."

Juliana is also in charge of the school's education program. The aim is to connect birds and nature to different aspects of the children's lives. They'll first teach what little birds need to be healthy before asking, "And what do little children need to be healthy?" It helps the children understand that we are part of nature too. It's the humans that need help understanding this, not the birds. Juliana refers to a quote on a *Parque* poster: "Nature does not need us, but we need nature." When she received a letter from a child saying, "I made a new friend today—the toucan!" she knew she was doing a good job.

Parque das Aves was in the process of hiring five new environmental educators and wardens when I was there. It will be their role to help educate and inspire the hundreds of thousands of tourists that visit *the park* every year.

4. Accept unexpected hospitality and be open to new experiences

Everywhere I went in Brazil hospitality was extended to me that I hadn't necessarily sought out or expected. This greatly enriched my time there—from Geraldo's impromptu trip with me into central Salvador to revel in the last day of Carnival, to Bia taking me all around town after visiting her nail bar, to Ilya and his jolly team showing me around São Paulo after visiting their start-up space.

One of the most enjoyable was my adventure to the remote Marau Peninsula in the Northeast. The first ferry left Salvador at 8:30 a.m. and I was supposed to be on that one. But I just missed it. It's a good thing I did.

On the next ferry I met some British expats: Lewis, Chloë, and her daughter Anna, who all turned out to be going the same way. Cholë, who used to be a nurse in London, decided to switch her life for another. She'd spent the previous five years building a beautiful lodge called Butterfly House (http://butterflyhousebahia.com) just next door to where I was staying. It turned out to be Chloë's birthday so of course there was a party at Butterfly House and I was kindly invited. What else would you expect from the social butterfly of Butterfly House?

After getting slightly lost on a deserted beach, I arrived in time for Lewis's signature caiprioska cocktail—just like a caipirinha but with vodka instead of cachaca. A couple of hours later we were doing shots of tequila. After gourmet *amuse bouches* from friendly head chef Ilious, there was a delicious homemade chocolate cake, and more alcohol. I was invited to stay the night in my own gorgeous double room to avoid getting lost on the way home.

Ilious had lived on Portobello Road in London and knew exactly how to make bacon and scrambled eggs for a wondering Englishman. And we finished off the birthday cake for dessert at breakfast.

I had a splendid time at the Butterfly House and highly recommend it to anyone looking for a slice of bohemian luxury on the Marau Peninsula.

5. Revere and revel in nature

In the home of the Amazon rainforest and some of the world's most famous beaches, nature is always on one's mind. But there's so much more than I'd anticipated. The vast natural treasure of the *Pantanal*; the wonders of Iguaçu; sinkholes, caves, giant fish, and so many kinds of colourful birds! I've already talked about these wonders. Revelling in nature is a big part of any Brazilian adventure.

But even in one of its largest urban areas—Rio de Janeiro—nature is there to enjoy. And I just don't mean Sugar Loaf and the incomparable harbour view from atop Corcovado Mountain.

Five years ago, Caroline Neutzling started a blog about Brazilian *favelas*. She was studying in Rio and couldn't find a good source of information on what was really happening in poor communities so she started researching for herself: "I really needed to know what was going on from the people living there so I started to find out and write about it. I thought other people might be interested too."

They were. Enquiries started coming in through the blog and Caroline—or Cacá, as she prefers to be called—started a new, better kind of *favela* tour. There have always been such tours but in the past they were a kind of poverty safari with guides who knew little about the communities showing tourists around poor areas so they could take pictures. What Cacá did was vastly different. She set up a social enterprise tour agency called *Soul Brasileiro* to work with and for the communities she visited.

"Other *favela* tours have no integration with the local community, they just show the poverty. I wanted to do something different. There are over a 1,000 *favelas* and 20% of the national population lives in them. Each one has its own story, history, and community." *Soul Brasileiro* connected travellers with another perspective: the perspective of those who live in the community.

But wait—weren't we just talking about appreciating nature? How does this relate?

I joined Cacá and *Soul Brasileiro* on a four hour nature trail and a visit to *Favela Vale Encantado*. *Vale Encantado* is in the Tijuca Forest which is the largest urban forest in the world.

Residents care for this patch of jungle and run creative and sustainable projects to preserve its environment. We were guided by a local who told us that some families have lived in this area since the 1870s. Local families have practiced various trades for decades—from farming, to flower growing, to granite mining—and they have passed land ownership down through generations.

After our walk, we were treated to a cooked meal from their award-winning community-owned kitchen. Proceeds from meals and tours go towards setting up an organic food garden. So here, we've come full-circle with social development and nature linking together.

Unfortunately, *Soul Brasileiro* no longer operates today but other local residents do still operate tours. I recommend Gabriel Abreu who you can find via www.RichardBrownsdon.com.

Some of the other links and websites I have shared in this book might too, with time, cease to operate.

I hope I have given you the inspiration and ability to look for other amazing people to meet and great companies to work with on your adventures, if you can't find or connect with the ones I mention. Such is my ideal legacy for this book.

Conclusion

In the end, it all links together: the five regions, though so vast, are part of one landmass and country. The cultural and geographic areas, though so distinctive, share a common, rich, and complex history. Brazil's guardians—those wonderful change-makers I met with passion, perseverance, and visions of hope—may never meet each other; but they're all connected in their desire to make Brazil a better place.

As responsible eco-travellers open to learning and engaging with local people, we can connect, too. We can do far more than visit famous sites, snap pictures, and leave. We can connect with local people and learn from them. We can tell their stories and contribute to their causes. Maybe it's through writing a blog or an article. Maybe it's volunteering. Maybe it's donating funds to a great cause.

Whatever it is, we can do our best to make sure we give back more than we take.

I went to Brazil to find and share stories of amazing people and places that are having a positive impact on the planet. This was the heart and soul of Brazil I was hoping to find. I hope you find this too, wherever your adventures may take you.

My wish for you is to have many of your own inspiring adventures and to share these stories with the world.

Looking for more?

We want more too! You can read more adventures and see the photos that accompany this book at www.RichardBrownsdon. com but we also want to hear about your adventures.

If you have your own stories or have been inspired to create new ones, share them with us and other Inspiring Adventurers in our community.

Join us here:

facebook.com/InspiringAdventures

instagram.com/Inspiring_Adventures

twitter.com/InspAdventures

We can't wait to meet you there.

And don't forget to use your 20% discount for any Inspiring Adventures travel products (until December 31st 2016) using the promo code "INSPBOOK" on Amazon.com and Amazon. co.uk

See our product range at www.Inspiring-Adventures.com and enjoy!

Acknowledgements

I would like to thank everyone mentioned in this book, for giving me your time and stories. Thank you.

Thanks to all my friends and family for your support and encouragement.

I'd also like to thank Loretta Rose, Lorna Morris, Ben Keene, for inspiring and starting this book creation process.

And a big thanks to Ella Doidge for all your continued love and support.

Made in the USA
Lexington, KY
16 June 2018